The
Anger
&
Aggression
Workbook

Self-Assessments, Exercises
& Educational Handouts

John J. Liptak, EdD
Ester A. Leutenberg

Illustrated by
Amy L. Brodsky, LISW

Whole Person Associates
Duluth, Minnesota

Whole Person Associates
101 West 2nd Street, Suite 203
Duluth, MN 55802-5004

800-247-6789

Books@WholePerson.com
WholePerson.com

The Anger & Aggression Workbook
Self-Assessments, Exercises & Educational Handouts

Printed in the United States of America

Editorial Director: Carlene Sippola
Art Director: Joy Morgan Dey

Library of Congress Control Number: 2007931344
ISBN: 978-1-57025-220-4

Using This Book *(for the professional)*

What is the best way to learn to control feelings of anger and aggression? Over the last century many different workbooks, workshops and self-help systems have been designed to help people develop anger management abilities. In the past twenty years, many research studies have focused on the value of self-reflection and journaling as a way of exploring personal characteristics, identifying ineffective behaviors and examining thoughts and feelings that lead to ineffective behaviors. This book is unique in that it combines two powerful psychological tools for anger management: self-assessment and journaling.

The Anger & Aggression Workbook contains five separate sections that will help the participants learn more about themselves as well as how anger and aggression are impacting their lives:

Anger History Scale helps individuals identify whether they were affected by the anger and aggression that took place in their families or with their friends as children.

Anger Intensity Scale helps individuals to identify how prone they are to anger and how strong their feelings of anger are.

Anger Triggers Scale helps individuals identify problematic, irrational thoughts that cause or misdirect their anger.

Anger Expression Scale helps individuals identify their particular ways of expressing their anger to other people.

Anger Consequences Scale helps individuals identify the significance the impact of their anger on themselves and the people that are important in their careers and lives.

These sections serve as an avenue for individual self-reflection, as well as group experiences revolving around identified topics of importance. Each assessment includes directions for easy administration, scoring and interpretation. In addition, each section includes exploratory activities, reflective journaling activities and educational handouts to help participants to discover their habitual, ineffective methods of managing anger, and to explore new ways for bringing about self-healing.

The art of self-reflection goes back many centuries and is rooted in many of the world's greatest spiritual and philosophical traditions. Socrates, the ancient Greek philosopher, was known to walk the streets engaging the people he met in philosophical reflection and dialogue. He felt that this type of activity was so important in life that he proclaimed, "The unexamined life is not worth living!" The unexamined life is one in which the same routine is continually repeated without ever thinking about its meaning to one's life and how this life really could be lived. However, a structured reflection and examination of beliefs, assumptions, characteristics and patterns can provide a better understanding which can lead to a more satisfying life and career. A greater level of self-understanding about important life skills is often necessary to make positive, self-directed changes in the negative patterns that keep repeating throughout life. The assessments and exercises in this book can help promote this self-understanding. Through involvement in the in-depth activities, the participant claims ownership in the development of positive patterns.

Journaling is an extremely powerful tool for enhancing self-discovery, learning, transcending traditional problems, breaking ineffective life and career habits, and helping to heal from psychological traumas of the past. From a physical point of view, writing reduces stress and lower muscle tension, blood pressure and heart rate levels. Psychologically, writing reduces feelings of sadness, depression and general anxiety, and leads to a greater level of life satisfaction and optimism. Behaviorally, writing leads to enhanced social skills, emotional intelligence and creativity.

By combining reflective assessment and journaling, your participants will engage in a revolutionary method for reducing and managing their anger and aggression.

*Thanks to the following professionals
whose input in this book has been invaluable!*

Carol Butler, MS Ed, RN, C

Nancy Day, OT Reg (Ont.)

Kathy Khalsa, OTR/L

Kathy Liptak, Ed.D.

Michael O'Leary, MFT

Eileen Regen, M.Ed., CJE

Lucy Ritzic, OTR/L

The Assessments, Journaling Activities, and Handouts

Materials in the Assessments, Journaling Activities, and Educational Handouts sections in this book are reproducible and can be photocopied for participants' use. The assessments contained in this book focus on self-reported data and thus are similar to ones used by psychologists, counselors, therapists and career consultants. The accuracy and usefulness of the information provided is dependent on the truthful information that each participant provides about himself or herself. By being honest, participants help themselves to learn about their unproductive and ineffective patterns in their lives, and to uncover information that might be keeping them from being as happy or as successful as they might be.

An assessment instrument can provide participants with valuable information about themselves; however, these assessments cannot measure or identify everything. The assessments' purpose is not to pigeon-hole certain characteristics, but rather to allow participants to explore all of their characteristics. This book contains self-assessments and not tests. Tests measure knowledge or whether something is right or wrong. For the assessments in this book, there are no right or wrong answers. These assessments ask for personal opinions or attitudes about a topic of importance in the participant's career and life.

When administering the assessments in this workbook, remember that the items are generically written so that they will be applicable to a wide variety of people but will not account for every possible variable for every person. None of the assessments are specifically tailored to one person, so use the assessments to help participants identify negative themes in their lives and find ways to break the hold that these patterns and their effects have in life and in a career.

Advise the participants taking the assessments that they should not spend too much time trying to analyze the content of the questions; they should think about the questions in general and then spontaneously report how they feel about each one. Whatever the results of the assessment, encourage participants to talk about their findings and their feelings pertaining to what have they discovered about themselves. Talking about anger and aggression issues can be very therapeutic and beneficial.

Layout of the Book

The Anger and Aggression Workbook is designed to be used either independently or as part of an integrated curriculum. You may administer one of the assessments and the journaling exercises to an individual or a group with whom you are working, or you may administer a number of the assessments over one or more days.

This book includes the following reproducibles in all five sections:

- **Assessment Instruments** — Self-assessment inventories with scoring directions and interpretation materials. Group facilitators can choose one or more of the activities relevant to their participants.

- **Activity Handouts** — Practical questions and activities that prompt self-reflection and promote self-understanding. These questions and activities foster introspection and promote pro-social behaviors.

- **Reflective Questions for Journaling** — Self-exploration activities and journaling exercises specific to each assessment to enhance self-discovery, learning, and healing.

- **Educational Handouts** — Handouts designed to enhance instruction can be used individually or in groups to promote a positive understanding of anger and to provide positive reinforcement for effective anger management. They can be distributed, converted into masters for overheads or transparencies, or written down on a board and discussed.

Who should use this program?

This book has been designed as a practical tool for helping professionals, such as therapists, counselors, psychologists, teachers, and group leaders. Depending on the role of the professional using   and the specific group's needs, these sections can be used individually or combined for a more comprehensive approach.

Why use self-assessments?

Self-assessments are important in teaching various anger management skills because they help participants to engage in these ways:

- Become aware of the primary motivators that guide their behavior
- Explore and learn to "let go" of troublesome habits and behavioral patterns learned in childhood
- Explore the effects of unconscious childhood messages
- Gain insight and "a wake up call" for behavioral change
- Focus their thinking on behavioral goals for change
- Uncover resources they possess that can help them to cope better with problems and difficulties
- Explore their personal characteristics without judgment
- Be fully aware of their strengths and weaknesses

Because the assessments are presented in a straightforward and easy-to-use format, individuals can self-administer, score and interpret each assessment at their own pace.

Introduction for the Participant

You will get angry from time to time. It is a very normal, usually healthy, human emotion. Although anger can serve a vital function in protecting and defending you, it too frequently turns into rage or verbal and physical aggression. Often anger is suppressed. Anger can be a wonderful warning sign that something is wrong, but it can take an emotional and physical toll as well. Anger can interfere with your role as a parent, partner, worker, and friend. Therefore, it is very important to learn how to manage your anger.

If you are having problems with feelings of anger and physical aggression, you probably want to change. You may feel the need to control yourself and your emotions more effectively. However, you may not know how to control your anger. Anger management is much more than learning a few tools and techniques that you can use when you get upset. It is about getting to know yourself. It is learning what triggers your anger, ways you choose to express anger to others, consequences of your anger, incidents from your childhood that may lead to anger, and the level of intensity of your angry feelings.

Anger management experts believe that anger and aggression are primarily learned from people and events in your environment. Since you learned to feel angry, you can also learn other ways to react when you are angry. This book, *The Anger and Aggression Workbook*, is designed to help you learn about anger and aggression in your life and make constructive changes to better manage your own anger and aggression.

TABLE OF CONTENTS

Journaling Activities

Educational Handouts

SECTION III: Anger Triggers

Anger Triggers Scale

Cognitive Exercises 62

Journaling Activities

TABLE OF CONTENTS

SECTION I:
Anger History

Name_____

Date_____

Anger History Scale Directions

Are anger and aggression inherited or learned characteristics? Social learning theory suggests that as children we learn and exhibit behaviors modeled for us by significant people in our lives. Therefore, it is critical that you explore the anger and aggressive behaviors that you were exposed to as a child. The Anger History Scale can help you identify whether you were affected by the anger and aggression that took place in your relationships with family and friends during your early years, throughout your childhood, and into your adult years.

This assessment contains forty statements. Read each of the statements and decide if the statement is true or false. If it is true, circle the word **True** next to the statement. If the statement is false, circle the word **False** next to the statement. Ignore the letters after the True and False choices. They are for scoring purposes and will be used later. Do all forty items before going back to score this scale.

In the following example, the circled **False** indicates that the item is false for the participant completing the Anger History Scale:

While I was growing up, my mother / female caregiver showed her anger in these ways:

1. Destroyed things   True (1) (False (0))   Score _____

This is not a test and there are no right or wrong answers. Do not spend too much time thinking about your answers. Your initial response will be the most true for you. Be sure to respond to every statement.

(Turn to the next page and begin)

ANGER HISTORY SCALE

While I was growing up, my mother / female caregiver showed her anger in these ways:

1. Destroying things   True (1)   False (0)   Score _____

2. Locking me and / or my siblings in a closet   True (1)   False (0)   Score _____

3. Throwing things at me and / or other members of the family

    True (1)   False (0)   Score _____

4. Sulking, pouting, and not speaking to members of the family

    True (1)   False (0)   Score _____

5. Slamming doors in the house   True (1)   False (0)   Score _____

6. Shouting a lot   True (1)   False (0)   Score _____

7. Intimidating me and / or other members of the family   True (1)   False (0)   Score _____

8. Fighting often with my father / male caregiver   True (1)   False (0)   Score _____

9. Cursing and insulting me and / or the rest of the family

    True (1)   False (0)   Score _____

10. Spanking or beating me and / or my siblings   True (1)   False (0)   Score _____

        TOTAL _____

While I was growing up, my father / male caregiver showed his anger in these ways:

11. Destroying things   True (1)   False (0)   Score _____

12. Locking me and / or my siblings in a closet   True (1)   False (0)   Score _____

13. Throwing things at me and / or other members of the family

    True (1)   False (0)   Score _____

14. Sulking, pouting and not speaking to members of the family

    True (1)   False (0)   Score _____

15. Slamming doors in the house   True (1)   False (0)   Score _____

16. Shouting a lot   True (1)   False (0)   Score _____

17. Intimidating me and / or other members of the family   True (1)   False (0)   Score _____

18. Fighting often with my mother / female caregiver   True (1   False (0)   Score _____

19. Cursing and insulting me and / or the rest of the family

    True (1)   False (0)   Score _____

20. Spanking or beating me and / or my siblings   True (1)   False (0)   Score _____

        TOTAL _____

(Continued on the next page)

While I was growing up, my (circle one) brother, sister, grandfather, grandmother, uncle, aunt, teacher, other, showed her / his anger in these ways:

21. Destroying things — True (1) False (0) Score _____

22. Locking me and / or my siblings in a closet — True (1) False (0) Score _____

23. Throwing things at me and / or other members of the family — True (1) False (0) Score _____

24. Beating me and / or other members of the family — True (1) False (0) Score _____

25. Slamming doors in the house — True (1) False (0) Score _____

26. Shouting a lot — True (1) False (0) Score _____

27. Intimidating me and / or other members of the family — True (1) False (0) Score _____

28. Fighting with my mother / female caregiver — True (1) False (0) Score _____

29. Fighting with my father / male caregiver — True (1) False (0) Score _____

30. Cursing and insulting me and / or the other members of the family — True (1) False (0) Score _____

TOTAL _____

While I was growing up, my friends showed their anger in these ways:

31. Destroying things — True (1) False (0) Score _____

32. Hurting other children, physically and / or emotionally — True (1) False (0) Score _____

33. Throwing things at members of their family — True (1) False (0) Score _____

34. Beating other members of their family — True (1) False (0) Score _____

35. Slamming doors in their houses — True (1) False (0) Score _____

36. Shouting a lot — True (1) False (0) Score _____

37. Intimidating members of their family — True (1) False (0) Score _____

38. Fighting with their mother / female caregiver — True (1) False (0) Score _____

39. Fighting with their father / male caregiver — True (1) False (0) Score _____

40. Cursing and insulting their family — True (1) False (0) Score _____

TOTAL _____

(Go to the Scoring Directions on the next page)

Anger History Scale Scoring Directions

The Anger History Scale is designed to help you to identify how the anger and aggression that you were exposed to as a child may be affecting your current feelings of anger and aggression. To score this scale, you need to determine your scores on each of the individual scales and for the overall Anger History total.

To score the Anger History Scale:

Look at the forty items you just completed. Now you need to focus on numbers after each choice rather than the **True** or **False**. Total your score for each section.

Use the spaces below to transfer your scores to each of the scales below. Then total the scores and put that number in the **Total** column.

Mother / Female Caregiver Scale: Total Score from #1 through #10 = _____

Father / Male Caregiver Scale: Total Score from #11 through #20 = _____

Significant People Scale: Total Score from #21 through #30 = _____

Friends Scale: Total Score from #31 through #40 = _____

Add together all of the "Totals" from the individual scales to receive your
Anger History Total and write that number in the blank below:

Anger History Total   _____

(The Profile Interpretation section on the next page can help you interpret your scores)

Anger History Scale Profile Interpretation

INDIVIDUAL SCALE SCORE	TOTAL SCORES FOR ALL FOUR	RESULT	INDICATIONS
0 to 3	0 to 12	**low**	You have not been exposed to a great deal of anger and aggression when you were growing up. You probably did not experience a lot of fighting, shouting and physical violence among your family members and your friends.
4 to 6	13 t0 27	**moderate**	You have been exposed to some anger and aggressive behaviors when you were growing up.
7 to 10	28 to 40	**high**	You have been exposed to a great deal of anger and aggression when you were growing up. You possibly experienced a lot of fighting, shouting, withdrawing and physical violence among your family members and your friends.

The higher your score on the Anger History Scale, the more exposure you have had to anger and aggression, and thus are more prone to exhibit those feelings and behaviors yourself. In the areas in which you score in the Moderate or High range you should make efforts to explore your childhood and develop anger management skills. No matter if you scored Low, Moderate or High, the exercises and activities that follow are designed to help you to explore any anger and aggression you experienced while growing up.

Life History

Complete the following questions about your life and your attempts to cope with your anger and aggression. When you have answered all of the questions, look for self-defeating patterns that keep reoccurring in your life.

1) How would you describe your mother / female caregiver?

_____

_____

_____

2) How would you describe your father / male caregiver?

_____

_____

_____

3) How would you describe your siblings and your relationship with them?

_____

_____

_____

4) How would you describe your relationship with your parents / caregivers?

_____

_____

_____

5) How would you describe the relationship between your mother and your father?

_____

_____

_____

_____

(Continued on the next page)

(Life History continued)

6) How did your mother / female caregiver show her feelings of anger?

_____

_____

_____

_____

7) How did your father / male caregiver show his feelings of anger?

_____

_____

_____

_____

8) How did your brothers and sisters show their feelings of anger?

_____

_____

_____

_____

9) How would you describe your image of a typical relationship between a man and a woman?

_____

_____

_____

_____

10) How would you describe the way you expressed your anger as a child?

_____

_____

_____

_____

(Continued on the next page)

(Life History continued)

11) What positive experiences happened to you during your childhood?

_____

_____

_____

12) What negative anger-related experiences happened to you during your childhood?

_____

_____

_____

13) What types of anger and aggression problems did your parents / caregivers have?

_____

_____

_____

14) How is your anger-related style similar to that of your parents / caregivers?

_____

_____

_____

15) How do the anger and aggression style of your parents / caregivers affect you now?

_____

_____

_____

16) Review your responses. What patterns have you discovered?

_____

_____

_____

Blaming

Many different events or situations took place in your family when you were young that had an impact on you and who you are now. Your family, friends and culture influence your current beliefs about anger and aggression as well as they influence your angry and aggressive behaviors. However, it is important to find a way to alter your belief system so that you can function effectively in society.

Here are some basics about blaming:

Blame is the best way to stay in a problem. By blaming others, you give away all of your power to them. You often hold onto unresolved conflicts that help to sabotage your life. There comes a time when you have to give up angry feelings and stop feeling sorry for yourself. Now is that time! You have to stop blaming others for your problems and feelings. You need to take control of your life. Blaming others takes away from your ability to take action.

The past cannot be changed. In reality, your past is gone and is alive only in your mind. When you live in the past, you are merely experiencing your memories of the situation, not the actual situation. You can take another look at the past through healthier eyes and reinterpret the memories by looking at them differently. Looking at your past differently can help you to see your true self and to see your negative self-image as an illusion.

When you blame others for the unhappiness in your life, you do not take responsibility for your emotions. For example, instead of taking responsibility for your current job situation, you may still be thinking "My girlfriend made me do it" or "If it weren't for my boss, I would not be in this situation." By blaming others, you only depress yourself and decrease your motivation to reach your dreams. You need to start taking full responsibility for all that happens to you from this point forward.

People I Blame

Overcoming anger is about moving on from your past, no matter how difficult it has been. At this stage, you need to go back and re-examine your life in a new light. You need to start acting rather than reacting. When you react, you are at the mercy of other people and events. When you act, you are in control of your own life. By taking a look at the people who you blame for your current situation, you can learn to forgive and begin to let go of your anger.

People I blame for my current situation

Person I blame	Why do I blame this person?
1.	
2.	
3.	
4.	
5.	

People Who Have Hurt Me

Person who has hurt me	How this person has hurt me	How I feel about this person now
1.		
2.		
3.		
4.		
5.		

Forgive and Forget

When you are unable to forgive, you hurt nobody but yourself. Hatred and vengeance keep you emotionally imprisoned with feelings and thoughts that are out of your control. These thoughts and feelings cloud your perception of situations, events, and other people. It keeps your thoughts focused on the negative rather than the positive. You hold on to your old emotions and thoughts of revenge so that you can feel sorry for yourself. These old emotions cause you to feel tired, frustrated, and depressed. You need to release all of the negative thoughts and feelings—sadness, fear, jealousy, hurt, and anger—that are harming you now. Having released the old feelings allows you to receive new, positive emotions.

The best way to let go of old, painful thoughts and feelings is through forgiveness. Through forgiveness, you are able to release these negative sentiments and fill yourself with peace and serenity. If you allow yourself to be a victim based on pain and hardship you have endured in the past, you cannot gain control over your thoughts, feelings, and actions. You must be ready to forgive completely those who have hurt you.

To let go of the pain in your life you must be willing to forgive yourself and others. Only when you forgive can you move forward. If you are unable to forgive, you will always be stuck with the anger, pain, and frustration of the moment. While harboring this pain, you will not notice any love and kindness directed toward you. You will be too busy wrapped up in the pain and the anger.

Forgiveness

Write a statement forgiving people from your past:

I forgive my mother/female caregiver for:

_____

_____

I forgive my father/male caregiver for:

_____

_____

I forgive my significant others for:

_____

_____

I forgive my friends for:

_____

_____

Understanding Your Anger

Anger and aggression are not illnesses; they are a series of learned behaviors and poor choices. The following Anger Log allows you to keep track of your thoughts, feelings and behaviors related to your anger and aggression. Think back to a time when you were angry and complete the following Anger Log. Photocopy this page before you begin to write so that you can continue to track your aggressive behaviors in the future.

Anger History Log

Name_____   Date_____

The episode of anger was: _____

_____

_____

_____

When I got angry: _____

_____

_____

_____

_____

Why I got angry: _____

_____

_____

_____

_____

Beliefs that triggered the anger: _____

_____

_____

_____

_____

(Continued on the next page)

SECTION I: EXERCISES FOR UNDERSTANDING YOUR ANGER

(Anger History Log continued)

How I showed my anger: _____
_____
_____
_____
_____

Ways in which I tried to manage my anger: _____
_____
_____
_____
_____

What worked with how I managed my anger: _____
_____
_____
_____
_____

What did not work, with how I managed my anger: _____
_____
_____
_____
_____

How I will improve on my anger management approach in the future: _____
_____
_____
_____
_____

Anger and Aggressive Feelings

In what ways have your anger and aggressive feelings increased or decreased since you were a child?

_____

_____

_____

_____

_____

_____

_____

_____

_____

_____

_____

_____

_____

_____

_____

_____

_____

_____

_____

_____

_____

_____

Verbal and Nonverbal Messages

Verbal and nonverbal messages you received as a child may have affected your anger and aggression as an adult. Describe some of the messages about anger and aggression you received as a child.

_____

_____

_____

_____

_____

_____

_____

_____

_____

_____

_____

_____

_____

_____

_____

_____

_____

_____

_____

_____

_____

_____

_____

_____

© 2008 WHOLE PERSON ASSOCIATES, 101 W. 2ND ST., SUITE 203, DULUTH MN 55802 ▪ 800-247-6789

Anger History and Anger Today

Describe the similarities you see between your anger history and how you deal with feelings of anger today.

_____

_____

_____

_____

_____

_____

_____

_____

_____

_____

_____

_____

_____

_____

_____

_____

_____

_____

_____

_____

Anger Management Process

- Identify irrational attitudes & beliefs that predispose you to excessive anger

- Identify factors from childhood that prevent you from expressing anger effectively

- Forgive those who have hurt you with expressions of anger

- Learn appropriate ways to express anger to others

Physiological Signs of Anger

- Heart beating faster

- Breathing rate increases

- Fists clenched

- Face feels hot or cold

- Hands shaking

- Profuse sweating

- Higher body temperature

- Sudden dry mouth

- Stuttering

- Muscles tensing

- Goosebumps

- Face turns pale or red

- Teeth grinding, jaw clenching

Problems With Suppressing Anger

- Start suffering from depression

- Begin to have lower self-esteem

- Suffer from anxiety attacks

- Hide behind drugs or alcohol

- Hurt yourself or others

- Hate yourself

- Explode

SECTION II:
Anger Intensity

Name_____

Date_____

Anger Intensity Scale Directions

Anger is a very normal, healthy emotion that all of us feel. However, when it breaks out of control and becomes destructive, you may start experiencing problems at work, in your relationships, and in other aspects of your life. Because it is such a powerful emotion, you may have difficulty when you try to suppress or control it.

The Anger Intensity Scale can help you explore how prone you are to anger and how intense your angry feelings are. This scale contains thirty-two statements. Read each of the statements and decide how much you agree with the statement. In each of the choices listed, circle the number of your response on the line to the right of each statement.

In the following example, the circled 4 indicates that the statement is very true of the person completing the scale:

	VERY TRUE	TRUE	SOMEWHAT TRUE	NOT TRUE
1. I tend to become angry more frequently than others	(4)	3	2	1

This is not a test and there are no right or wrong answers. Do not spend too much time thinking about your answers. Your initial response will be the most true for you. Be sure to respond to every statement.

(Turn to the next page and begin)

Anger Intensity Scale

	VERY TRUE	TRUE	SOMEWHAT TRUE	NOT TRUE
1. I tend to become angry more frequently than others	4	3	2	1
2. I am often critical of others	4	3	2	1
3. I become angry when other people let me down	4	3	2	1
4. I hit others when I become angry	4	3	2	1
5. I tend to become angrier than others in the same situation	4	3	2	1
6. I often make cutting remarks to others	4	3	2	1
7. I become angry when I do dumb things	4	3	2	1
8. I damage property when I become angry	4	3	2	1
9. It is easy to make me angry	4	3	2	1
10. I can be very sarcastic	4	3	2	1
11. I become angry when things do not go as I planned	4	3	2	1
12. I often slam doors behind me when I am angry	4	3	2	1
13. I become angry at least once every day	4	3	2	1
14. I often yell at other people	4	3	2	1
15. I become angry if someone embarrasses me	4	3	2	1
16. I find myself banging on things to gain people's attention	4	3	2	1
17. When I become angry I stay angry for a long time	4	3	2	1
18. I say hateful things to other people	4	3	2	1
19. I become angry around incompetent people	4	3	2	1
20. Sometimes I cannot control my urge to hurt others	4	3	2	1
21. I often feel more angry than I should	4	3	2	1
22. I often swear at other people	4	3	2	1
23. I become angry when others do not give me enough credit	4	3	2	1
24. When I am really angry, I am capable of slapping someone	4	3	2	1
25. I often become angry for no specific reason	4	3	2	1
26. I like to argue with other people	4	3	2	1
27. I become angry when things do not go my way	4	3	2	1
28. I break things when I become angry	4	3	2	1
29. I am unable to control my feelings when I become angry	4	3	2	1
30. I sometimes spread gossip about people I do not like	4	3	2	1
31. I become angry when life gives me "a raw deal"	4	3	2	1
32. I often enter into physical confrontations with other people	4	3	2	1

(Go to scoring on the next page)

Anger Intensity Scale Scoring

People become angry for a variety of reasons. The purpose of this assessment is to help you explore how the intensity of your anger builds and in what situation your anger erupts. The Anger Intensity Scale is designed to measure the intensity of your anger. Four different areas of anger management have been identified that make up this scale:

- Anger Arousal
- Verbal
- Environmental
- Hostility

The meaning of each scale will be presented after the scoring. The scoring process groups items into those four scales so you can explore your own anger intensity profile.

Use the spaces below to record the number which you circled on each individual item of the assessment.

RAW SCORE	RAW SCORE	RAW SCORE	RAW SCORE
1_____	2_____	3_____	4_____
5_____	6_____	7_____	8_____
9_____	10_____	11_____	12_____
13_____	14_____	15_____	16_____
17_____	18_____	19_____	20_____
21_____	22_____	23_____	24_____
25_____	26_____	27_____	28_____
29_____	30_____	31_____	32_____
Anger Arousal	**Verbal**	**Environmental**	**Hostility**
Total = _____	Total = _____	Total = _____	Total = _____

(Go to the Profile Interpretation on the next page)

Anger Intensity Scale Profile Interpretation

Anger tends to be a natural, adaptive way to respond to threats in your life. Used effectively, it can help you to respond powerfully and defend yourself when you are attacked. A certain amount of anger is necessary for survival. However, too much anger can cause you and the people around you many problems. Look at the profile interpretation materials below. For each of the scales identify whether you rated low, average, or high in each of the anger intensity scales.

TOTAL SCALES SCORES	RESULT	INDICATIONS
8 to 15	**fairly low**	You tend to have few problems with angry feelings.
16 to 24	**moderate**	Your anger intenesity level is moderate.
25 to 32	**high**	Your anger intensity level is high. Your angry outbursts are probably causing many problems in your life and job.

Now look at the pages that follow and read more about the specific scales on which you scored in the low or moderate ranges. Whether you scored low, moderate or high, you will benefit from doing the exercises on the following pages.

Anger Intensity Scale Descriptions

Anger Arousal Scale

People scoring high on this scale tend to become angrily aroused very easily and quickly each day, and often they stay angry for a very long period of time. Often they become angry for no specific reason and are unable to control their feelings.

Verbal Scale

People scoring high on this scale tend to be critical of others. They often make hurtful remarks to other people and are very sarcastic. They will yell at others, swear, and say hateful things when they become angry. They are people who like to argue and are prone to gossiping about others.

Environmental Scale

People scoring high on this scale tend to become angered by other people. They are upset if others let them down and if things do not go as planned. They become angry if they are embarrassed and when they work with incompetent people in the community. They like things to go their way and resort to anger if they do not.

Hostility Scale

People scoring high on this scale tend to become physically abusive when they become angry. They may hit other people, do damage to property, bang on a table until they achieve what they want, or punch, hit or slap other people. They typically break things and become physically abusive.

Anger can manifest itself in a variety of ways. Remember that a little bit of anger can be positive and helpful, but too much anger can affect your general wellness, your health, your job and your relationships. The following exercises have been designed to help you manage your anger. Try doing all of the anger management exercises that follow, then practice the ones with which you feel most comfortable, no matter how you scored, low, moderate or high.

Breathing

Because breath is vital to life itself, proper breathing is very important and can be an excellent form of stress reduction. The pace at which you breathe and the depth of your breathing is vital in relaxation and stress reduction. When you encounter stressful situations, your breathing quickens and becomes more shallow. Breathing can also help to relax and quiet your body. Diaphragmatic breathing, in which you take in long, very deep breaths, is an especially powerful tool for relaxation. In diaphragmatic breathing, you push out your stomach and draw in a long deep breath. Then you exhale as slowly and as long as possible. Repeat this until relaxation occurs.

Experiential Exercise — Breathing

Pay attention to your breathing. Do not try to change it, but just become more aware of it. This will allow you to easily be brought into conscious awareness. Make note of the parts of your body or ways your mind is attempting to interfere with the natural movement of your breathing. If your attention wanders and takes you away from the focus on your breathing, simply bring back your attention so that you return to your focus. Dwell on the rise and fall of your chest as you inhale and exhale. Simply allow your attention to settle you and stop distracting thoughts.

What do you notice about your breathing as you begin to attend to it?

_____

_____

_____

_____

_____

_____

_____

_____

_____

_____

_____

Aerobic Exercise

Aerobic exercise helps the body by releasing chemicals, called endorphins, into your brain. When this occurs, your body is able to return quickly to normal, leaving you feeling refreshed and relaxed. Aerobic exercise uses sustained, rhythmic activity involving primarily the large muscles in your legs. Aerobic exercises include such activities as jogging, running, brisk walking, jumping rope, skiing, swimming, bicycling, kickboxing, or other high intensity martial arts and aerobic training.

What types of aerobic exercises do you currently engage in that might help you manage your anger?

_____

_____

_____

_____

_____

_____

What types of aerobic exercises do you want to engage in to help you manage your anger?

_____

_____

_____

_____

_____

_____

What steps do you need to take to become involved in one of these exercises?

_____

_____

_____

_____

_____

Progressive Muscle Relaxation

Progressive muscle relaxation helps you to bring relaxation to all parts of your body through concentrated awareness. This relaxation helps to reduce anger and provides you with a system for stopping the escalation of anger in your daily life. Progressive relaxation allows you to actually produce relaxation by focusing self-suggestions of warmth and relaxation in specific muscle groups throughout the body.

Experiential Exercise — Progressive Muscle Relaxation

Sit in a comfortable position. Close your eyes and start to feel your body relaxing. Think of yourself as a rag doll. Let the relaxation pass through each organ and body part. In this exercise, start with your feet and progressively relax each part of your body. This will help you to manage your stress effectively. Begin by having your body progressively relax with such statements as:

"I am relaxing my feet.....	*My feet are warm.....*	*My feet are relaxed."*
"I am relaxing my ankles.....	*My ankles are warm.....*	*My ankles are relaxed."*
"I am relaxing my calves.....	*My calves are warm.....*	*My calves are relaxed."*
"I am relaxing my knees.....	*My knees are warm.....*	*My knees are relaxed."*
"I am relaxing my thighs.....	*My thighs are warm.....*	*My thighs are relaxed."*

Do this with the rest of your body until you are totally relaxed from your head to your feet. Block any distractions out of your mind as you concentrate on relaxing your entire body.

Meditation

Meditation is the practice of attempting to focus your attention on one thing at a time. It is a method in which you use repeated mental focus to quiet your mind, which in turn quiets your body. In meditation, focusing on one thing allows your mind to stay concentrated and excludes all other thoughts. There are many different forms of meditation. In meditation you can focus by repeating a word like "OM," count your breaths by saying "one," "two," "three" after you exhale with each breath, or gaze at an object like a candle or a piece of wood without thinking about it in words.

Thought Control

Whenever you start to feel angry, you can examine your thinking by first stopping what you are saying and doing. Do not push your thoughts away or ignore them, simply stop in your tracks. Then you want to explore what you are saying to yourself. Remember that what you say to yourself can either calm you down or make you angrier.

Do not say powerless, victim-affirming statements like these:

"Who is he or she to treat me like this?"

"Life's not fair."

"Just my luck."

"This is not fair."

"This should not be happening to me."

"I don't deserve this."

Say powerful, self-sufficient, self-empowerment statements like these:

"I don't have to take this personally."

"They are entitled to their opinion."

"I will react differently this time."

"This is a challenge, not a problem."

"Life isn't always fair."

"These types of things happen to all people."

Listen to Music

Listening to music is probably one of the best forms of relaxation because it is so accessible. To benefit from the relaxation of music, select music that is soothing and that you find peaceful. To benefit the most from your music relaxation sessions, find approximately one-half hour of uninterrupted time to be by yourself daily.

What type of music would be relaxing for you?

_____

_____

_____

Identify Physical Signs

Start to track the physical signs and symptoms that occur just before you begin to feel angry. These warning signals may include such things as rapid breathing and increased pulse rate.

Anger-Producing Situations	Physical Signs & Symptoms

Keep an Anger Diary

It would be helpful to keep a record of when you become angry, what situation brings the feelings on, and whom you are with. This exercise will help you identify patterns of anger and hostility.

When did I bcome angry?	What was the situation?	Who was with me?

(Continued on the next page)

Anger Intensity Log

Date _____   Time_____

Brief Description of the event _____

_____

_____

_____

Degree of anger (1 = low, 10 = high): _____

Stress in my life at the time _____

_____

_____

_____

Thoughts that might trigger the anger _____

_____

_____

_____

Results of anger _____

_____

_____

_____

What I will do next time _____

_____

_____

_____

Humor

One way to stop your anger from escalating is to look at the light side of the anger-producing situation. One way to do this is to think about the absurdity of the situation and try to find humor in it. By poking fun at things, you will be able to reframe the anger as something less serious and not deserving of angry feelings.

Experiential Exercise — Humor

Close your eyes and imagine a situation in which you find yourself becoming angry. This might be a situation like waiting in a long line in the grocery store, doing poorly at work, or receiving a parking ticket. About thirty seconds after you begin to think about the situation, try to imagine how silly the situation really is. Try to find humor in the situation.

What situation makes you angry?

_____

_____

How can you view the situation with more humor and how did it affect your angry feelings?

_____

_____

Recreation

Recreational activities can also help you to reduce the anger you experience. By engaging in active, challenging recreational activities you will find yourself experiencing less anger.

What types of recreational activities do you enjoy?

_____

_____

_____

What types of recreational activities might help you reduce feelings of anger?

_____

_____

_____

Intense and Destructive Anger

Write about one time when anger became too intense and destructive in your life.

_____

_____

_____

_____

_____

_____

_____

_____

_____

_____

_____

_____

_____

_____

_____

_____

_____

_____

_____

_____

_____

_____

_____

Reducing Intensity of Angry Feelings

Write about steps that you might take to reduce the intensity of your angry feelings when an anger-producing situation or event occurs.

_____

_____

_____

_____

_____

_____

_____

_____

_____

_____

_____

_____

_____

_____

_____

_____

_____

_____

_____

_____

_____

_____

_____

Angry Words Hurt People

Describe an event in which you used words to hurt another person when you were angry.

_____

_____

_____

_____

_____

_____

_____

_____

_____

_____

_____

_____

_____

_____

_____

_____

_____

_____

_____

_____

_____

Physical Reactions Accompanying Anger

- Teeth clenching

- Skin hot and red

- Loss of appetite or overeating

- Acne

- Fatigue

- Migraine headaches

- Neck pain

- Stomachache

- Sleeping too much or inability to sleep

Health Consequences of Anger

- Heart disease

- Cancer

- Rheumatoid arthritis

- Psoriasis

- Ulcers or other stomach problems

- Epilepsy

- Raynaud's disease

- High blood pressure

 © 2008 WHOLE PERSON ASSOCIATES, 101 W. 2ND ST., SUITE 203, DULUTH MN 55802 ▪ 800-247-6789

Blowing Off Anger in a Healthy Manner

- Recognize the anger for what it is

- Determine what made you so angry

- Stop before you act

- Calm down by counting to thirty

- Take a deep breath

- Think about what you want to say

- Tell the person how you are feeling

- Try to negotiate

SECTION III:
Anger Triggers

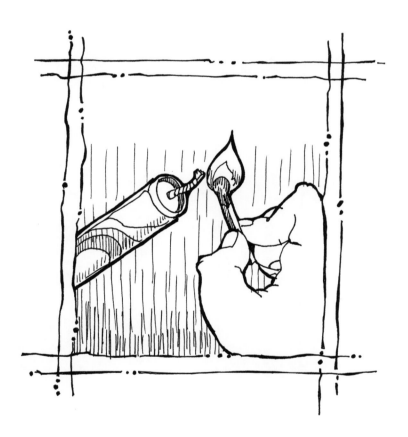

Name_____

Date_____

Anger Triggers Scale Directions

Cognitive psychologists believe that it is not a situation or another person that causes anger. They suggest that your emotions are actually the consequence of what you think about an event. When something happens to you, you begin to think about what happened, you make an evaluation, and then emotions occur. Therefore, you can change your emotions by changing how you think in a variety of situations.

This assessment contains thirty statements related to what sets off your emotions. Read each of the statements and decide whether or not the statement describes you. If the statement does describe you, circle the number in the YES column. If the statement does not describe you, circle the number in the NO column.

In the following example, the circled number under "Yes" indicates the statement is descriptive of the person completing the inventory.

	YES	**NO**	
I am considered inflexible	(2)	1	(S)

This is not a test and there are no right or wrong answers. Do not spend too much time thinking about your answers. Your initial response will be the most true for you. Be sure to respond to every statement.

(Turn to the next page and begin)

Anger Triggers Scale

	YES	NO		
I am considered inflexible	2	1	(S)	
I listen to the opinions of others	1	2	(S)	
I think too critically about myself	2	1	(S)	
I am uncomfortable when I am not in control of things	2	1	(S)	
I worry about my public image too much	2	1	(S)	
I don't care if I have a perfect reputation	2	1	(S)	
I have a great desire to appear successful	2	1	(S)	
I become upset if I cannot do something as well as I want	2	1	(S)	
I am rarely satisfied	2	1	(S)	
I do not become angry when I am late for anything	1	2	(S)	TOTAL _____
I become angry when others are unfair	2	1	(O)	
I become upset if others are late	2	1	(O)	
When someone speaks ill of me, I become angry	2	1	(O)	
I worry when someone makes a decision that affects me	2	1	(O)	
I do not like to point out mistakes made by others	1	2	(O)	
I don't receive feedback from others well	2	1	(O)	
When I express my opinions, I become upset if others disagree	2	1	(O)	
I become angry when others make noises that interrupt me	2	1	(O)	
I become angry when others do not give me the credit I deserve	2	1	(O)	
I am rarely impatient with people who do not do their job well	1	2	(O)	TOTAL _____
I become angry if my car breaks down	2	1	(W)	
I rarely become angry if I am caught in traffic	1	2	(W)	
I become angry if events do not go as I plan	2	1	(W)	
I become angry if I cannot get somewhere quickly enough	2	1	(W)	
I become angry when technology does not work	2	1	(W)	
I become angry if the weather interferes with my activities	2	1	(W)	
I become irritated when things are not done quickly enough	2	1	(W)	
I become angry when businesses are disorganized	2	1	(W)	
I rarely become angry when I have to wait in line	1	2	(W)	
I do not like to compare myself with other people	1	2	(W)	TOTAL _____

(Go to the Scoring Directions on the next page)

Anger Triggers Scale Scoring Directions

The Anger Triggers Scale is designed to help you identify your problematic irrational thoughts that cause or misdirect your anger. For the items on the previous two pages, add the numbers that you circled, which are indicated with an (S). This will allow you to receive your Expectations of Self score. You will receive a total in the range from 10 to 20. Put that number in the space marked next to the Expectations of Self Total below. Do the same for the other two scales: (O) – Expectations of Others score, and (W) – Expectations about the World score. Then, transfer these totals to the spaces below.

(S) Expectations of Self Total = _____

(O) Expectations of Others Total = _____

(W) Expectations about the World Total = _____

To receive your overall Anger Triggers total, add together the three scores above. Total scores range from 30 to 60. Put that score in the space provided below.

ANGER TRIGGERS TOTAL = _____

Profile Interpretation

INDIVIDUAL SCALE SCORE	TOTAL FOR ALL THREE SCALES	RESULT	INDICATIONS
10 to 13	30 to 39	**low**	You do not have many irrational thoughts causing you to become angry.
14 to 16	40 to 50	**moderate**	You have some irrational thoughts that cause you anger, but not too many to be harmful in your life and in your job.
17 to 20	51 to 60	**high**	You have many irrational thoughts that are causing you to become angry.

No matter how you scored on the Anger Triggers Scale Low, Moderate or High, you will benefit from doing all of the following exercises.

Cognitive Exercises

The following exercises were designed to help you explore your irrational and distorted thinking, and to help you to make changes so that you can begin to think and react more realistically.

Our Thinking Determines Our Feelings

How we react emotionally often depends on our thinking. When we become angry, many times it is because of our expectations for a situation. You must begin to examine your thought patterns to understand what is triggering your angry feelings. These thought patterns are often referred to as self-talk. Self-talk includes the words that pop into your head as if you were having a conversation with yourself. By understanding the self-talk that is prompting your anger, you can change your ways of thinking that often result in angry feelings. You need to learn to let go of certain types of thinking if you are going to control your anger.

You learned to think in these irrational ways just as you learned to speak a language or play a sport. If you learned to think irrationally, you can learn new thinking patterns too. To break this habit, you need to learn new habits!

Angry Situations

Why do some people become angry about certain situations, yet others do not? Some people are able to stay calm in certain situations, while other people would break into an uncontrollable rage. Some situations cause us to feel personally attacked while others do not. Many different events and situations trigger anger. What triggers each person's anger is unique, based on what you have come to expect of yourself, of other people and of the world in general. It is important for you to explore and revise your unrealistic and irrational expectations of yourself, of others and of the world around you.

Expectations of Myself

Irrational expectations that you have about yourself can definitely affect your feelings of anger. Complete the following exercise to explore the irrational expectations you have about yourself.

Irrational Expectations of Myself	Feelings Caused by These Expectations

Expectations of Self

Physical Performance

Describe the sports or other physical tasks in which you expect more than you can deliver.

_____

_____

_____

How can you alter your thinking so that you are more realistic?

_____

_____

_____

Intellectual Pursuits

Describe the intellectual tasks in which you expect more of yourself than you can deliver.

_____

_____

_____

How can you alter your thinking so that you are more realistic?

_____

_____

_____

Deadlines

Describe the situations in which you have deadlines when you expect more of yourself than you can deliver.

_____

_____

_____

_____

(Continued on the next page)

(Expectations of Self – Deadlines continued)

How can you alter your thinking so that you are more realistic?

_____

_____

_____

Successes / Achievements

Describe the areas of success and achievements in which you expect more of yourself than you can deliver.

_____

_____

_____

_____

How can you alter your thinking so that you are more realistic?

_____

_____

_____

_____

Spirituality

Describe the spiritual tasks in which you expect more of yourself than you can deliver.

_____

_____

_____

_____

How can you alter your thinking so that you are more realistic?

_____

_____

_____

_____

Expectations of Others

Irrational expectations that you have of others can definitely affect your feelings of anger.
Complete the following exercise to explore the irrational expectations you have of other people.

Irrational Expectations of Others	Feelings Caused by These Expectations

(Continued on the next page)

© 2008 WHOLE PERSON ASSOCIATES, 101 W. 2ND ST., SUITE 203, DULUTH MN 55802 ▪ 800-247-6789

(Expectations of Others continued)

Manners

Describe the unwritten rules of etiquette people break that make you angry.

_____

_____

_____

_____

How can you alter your thinking so that you are more realistic?

_____

_____

_____

_____

Disappointments

Describe the disappointing things people do that evoke your anger.

_____

_____

_____

_____

How can you alter your thinking so that you are more realistic?

_____

_____

_____

_____

Support

Describe how a lack of support from others causes you to be angry.

_____

_____

_____

_____

(Continued on the next page)

(Expectations of Others – Support continued)

How can you alter your thinking so that you are more realistic?

_____

_____

_____

_____

Intimacy

Describe how intimate situations can make you angry.

_____

_____

_____

_____

How can you alter your thinking so that you are more realistic?

_____

_____

_____

_____

Intrusions

Describe how intrusions on your time cause you to be angry.

_____

_____

_____

_____

How can you alter your thinking so that you are more realistic?

_____

_____

_____

_____

Expectations of the World

Irrational expectations that you have about the world can definitely affect your feelings of anger. Complete the following exercise to explore the irrational expectations you have about the world.

Irrational Expectations of the World	Feelings Caused by These Expectations

(Continued on the next page)

(Expectations of the World continued)

Electronic Devices

Describe how you become angry at computers and other electronic devices.

_____

_____

_____

_____

How can you alter your thinking so that you are more realistic?

_____

_____

_____

_____

Lack of Organization

Describe how things that are not organized to your liking irritate you.

_____

_____

_____

_____

How can you alter your thinking so that you are more realistic?

_____

_____

_____

_____

Unfolding

Describe the situations in which sudden changes cause you to be angry.

_____

_____

_____

_____

(Continued on the next page)

(Expectations of the World - Unfolding continued)

How can you alter your thinking so that you are more realistic?

_____

_____

_____

_____

Traffic

Describe how traffic conditions evoke your anger.

_____

_____

_____

_____

How can you alter your thinking so that you are more realistic?

_____

_____

_____

_____

Weather

Describe how changes in the weather upset you.

_____

_____

_____

_____

How can you alter your thinking so that you are more realistic?

_____

_____

_____

_____

Yourself and Triggers

Write what you have learned about yourself and the types of events and situations that trigger feelings of anger in you.

_____

_____

_____

_____

_____

_____

_____

_____

_____

_____

_____

_____

_____

_____

_____

_____

_____

_____

_____

_____

_____

_____

Feelings That Cause Pain and Disruption

Write how your feelings have caused you pain or disrupted your life.

_____

_____

_____

_____

_____

_____

_____

_____

_____

_____

_____

_____

_____

_____

_____

_____

_____

_____

_____

_____

_____

_____

_____

_____

_____

_____

Lessen and Eliminate Anger Triggers

What kinds of things can you do to lessen or eliminate the anger triggers in your life?

_____

_____

_____

_____

_____

_____

_____

_____

_____

_____

_____

_____

_____

_____

_____

_____

_____

_____

_____

_____

_____

_____

_____

Anger as a Secondary Emotion

Anger is often a cover-up for prior, stronger feelings including the following:

- Frustration

- Guilt

- Loneliness

- Fear

- Rejection

- Hurt

- Self-Doubt

Negative Things You Say to Yourself

- "This is not fair."

- "She makes me angry."

- "Life is unfair."

- "This only happens to me."

- "Why me?"

- "I should be happier."

- "If I could only...."

- "I'm in pain, I must be doing something wrong."

- "He should not have done that."

- "Just my luck."

Positive Things You Might Say to Yourself

- "No one can MAKE me feel angry.
  I control how I feel."

- "If I think more rationally, I'll feel better."

- "I choose to be responsible for
  my own behavior."

- "I am in control of my emotions."

- "I am okay..."

- "Life is not always going to be fair,
  but I can decide how I think, feel,
  and act."

- "I create my own luck."

- "I no longer let people push my buttons."

- "I cannot control other people, but I can
  control how I react to other people."

- "This is just a minor setback that
  I will overcome."

SECTION IV:
Anger Expression Style

Name_____

Date_____

Anger Expression-Style Scale Directions

No two people are exactly alike in expressing their anger. It is important that you become more aware of how you tend to express anger and the affect that this anger expression style has on your relationships, your job and your life.

To begin to manage your anger you must first become more aware of your anger expression style. The Anger Expression-Style Scale will help you identify your style in expressing anger toward other people. This scale can help you to see the connection between anger expressions and consequences of this expression style. You will learn more effective ways for expressing anger.

In the following example, the circled 3 indicates that the statement was somewhat descriptive of the person completing the scale.

4 = VERY DESCRIPTIVE	3 = SOMEWHAT DESCRIPTIVE	2 = A LITTLE DESCRIPTIVE	1 = NOT AT ALL DESCRIPTIVE

1. When I become angry I become silent because I know it bothers others.

4   (3)   2   1

This is not a test, and there are no right or wrong answers, do not spend too much time thinking about your answers. Your initial response will be the most true for you. Be sure to respond to every statement.

(Turn to the next page and begin)

Anger Expression-Style Scale

4 = VERY DESCRIPTIVE **3 = SOMEWHAT DESCRIPTIVE** **2 = A LITTLE DESCRIPTIVE** **1 = NOT AT ALL DESCRIPTIVE**

1. When I become angry I become silent because I know the silence bothers others. 4 3 2 1

2. I tend to sulk and feel sorry for myself .4 3 2 1

3. I pout when I don't get my way. 4 3 2 1

4. When I don't want to do something I procrastinate 4 3 2 1

5. I often say, "No, I'm fine," even though I am angry 4 3 2 1

6. I often deliberately avoid others so they will not bother me 4 3 2 1

7. I sometimes approach projects half-heartedly when I am angry 4 3 2 1

8. I find myself complaining about others behind their backs 4 3 2 1

9. I will deliberately refuse to do others a favor, knowing it will bother them 4 3 2 1

10. I feel a need to get even when I don't get my way. 4 3 2 1

A TOTAL = _____

11. I don't like others to know when I am angry. 4 3 2 1

12. Even if I am angry, I portray myself publicly as cool and collected . .4 3 2 1

13. I rarely share my problems or frustrations 4 3 2 1

14. I often let days pass by before mentioning my anger to someone. . .4 3 2 1

15. Others say that I am often depressed or moody 4 3 2 1

16. I am often resentful of others, but I rarely show it. 4 3 2 1

17. I suffer with many physical complaints including insomnia, stomach problems, and headaches 4 3 2 1

18. I sometimes feel paralyzed when I am in an unwanted situation 4 3 2 1

19. I rarely start conversations about troublesome topics 4 3 2 1

20. I hold my anger in until later 4 3 2 1

B TOTAL = _____

(Continued on the next page)

Anger Expression-Style Scale *(continued)*

4 = VERY DESCRIPTIVE	3 = SOMEWHAT DESCRIPTIVE	2 = A LITTLE DESCRIPTIVE	1 = NOT AT ALL DESCRIPTIVE

21. I am often blunt and forceful if someone frustrates me 4   3   2   1
22. I tend to express myself through yelling or violence 4   3   2   1
23. Others feel that I am difficult to get along with 4   3   2   1
24. I frequently am involved in fights. 4   3   2   1
25. I don't worry about others' feelings 4   3   2   1
26. I enjoy verbal disagreements with other people. 4   3   2   1
27. I often feel the need to dominate others 4   3   2   1
28. I express anger by breaking and throwing things. 4   3   2   1
29. When I am talking my voice often becomes increasingly louder. . . . 4   3   2   1
30. I find myself arguing with family and friends often 4   3   2   1

C TOTAL = _____

31. I often give in to other people 4   3   2   1
32. I feel like I am "walking on eggshells" around other people 4   3   2   1
33. I think it's my fault when others are rude to me 4   3   2   1
34. I will suffer silently rather than stand up for myself. 4   3   2   1
35. I find myself apologizing a lot of the time 4   3   2   1
36. I often do not express my honest feelings 4   3   2   1
37. I often do not express my true needs and wants 4   3   2   1
38. I often do not express my true thoughts and beliefs 4   3   2   1
39. When I talk to others, I often do not make eye contact with them   4   3   2   1
40. I usually let others have their way. 4   3   2   1

D TOTAL = _____

(Continued on to the next page)

Anger Expression-Style Scale (continued)

4 = VERY DESCRIPTIVE	3 = SOMEWHAT DESCRIPTIVE	2 = A LITTLE DESCRIPTIVE	1 = NOT AT ALL DESCRIPTIVE

41. I feel I have the right to my own opinions 4 3 2 1

42. I am respectful of others' opinions 4 3 2 1

43. I believe that I have the right to say NO to others 4 3 2 1

44. I can communicate my needs clearly to others. 4 3 2 1

45. I try to compromise so everybody will win 4 3 2 1

46. I can deal with situations without dominating them. 4 3 2 1

47. I am not responsible for justifying my behavior 4 3 2 1

48. I have the right to make mistakes 4 3 2 1

49. I usually tell people why I am angry at them 4 3 2 1

50. I can become angry at someone, yet not hurt them
    verbally or physically 4 3 2 1

E TOTAL = _____

Anger Expression-Style Scale Scoring Directions

The Anger Expression-Style Scale is designed to help people explore the way in which they tend to demonstrate their anger. This scale can help you to identify your specific style when it comes to expressing anger in your life. Add your scores within each section of this scale. Record each total in the space provided after each section.

TOTALS

A. _____ (Passive Aggressive)

B. _____ (Suppressing)

C. _____ (Open Aggressive)

D. _____ (Passive)

E. _____ (Assertive)

Profile Interpretation

TOTAL SCALES SCORES	RESULT	INDICATIONS
10 to 19	**low**	You do not use this particular anger expression style.
20 to 30	**moderate**	You may use this particular anger expression style some of the time but not all of the time.
31 to 49	**high**	You use this particular anger expression style a great deal of the time.

For scales which you scored in the Moderate or High range, find the descriptions on the pages that follow. Then, read the description and complete the exercises that are included. No matter how you scored, Low, Moderate or High, you will benefit from these exercises by developing more effective anger expression skills.

Anger Expression Styles

Passive Aggressive

In this style, you suppress your anger until you can express it later. You become angry, and you know you become angry, but you decide to frustrate others in more subtle, passive ways.

Assertive

In this style, you become angry with others and still are considerate of the needs and feelings of others. You will stick up for yourself and your beliefs, but not become angry if others do not agree with you.

Open Aggressive

In this style, you express your anger through openly aggressive words and behaviors. Open aggressive includes many aspects of anger including rage, intimidation and explosive anger. Open aggressive, however, can also include criticizing others, bickering and fighting verbally with others.

Suppressing

In this style, you are hesitant to admit your own anger. You have probably decided not to lower yourself to the expression of anger. When anger-producing situations occur, you put on a good front and pretend not to feel angry at all. You stuff your anger and hold it in until later.

Passive

In this style, you have a very difficult time standing up for yourself. You tend to have low self-esteem and believe that other people are always right. You have trouble asserting yourself with other people. You will give up some of your wants and needs to avoid others criticizing you.

Passive Aggressive Style

High scores on this scale suggest that you find a way to suppress your anger until you can express it later. You become angry, and you know you become angry but you decide to frustrate others in more subtle, passive ways. You have a need for control and a need to get the upper hand. One way you handle anger is by cleverly sabotaging the efforts of the person or people who make you angry.

In what ways do you find yourself being passively aggressive?

_____

_____

_____

In what situations do you find yourself becoming passively aggressive?

_____

_____

_____

What is usually the result of your passive aggressiveness?

_____

_____

_____

What frustrates you the most so that you become passive aggressive?

_____

_____

_____

Why have you been unable to control this passive aggression?

_____

_____

_____

Assertive Style

High scores on this scale suggest that you are able to become angry with others and yet still be considerate of the needs and feelings of others. You will stick up for yourself and your beliefs, but not become angry if others do not agree with you. You are able to take a stand in your relationships, communicate your emotions in a constructive manner and resolve conflicts effectively.

In what ways do you find yourself being assertive?

_____

_____

_____

In what situations do you find yourself becoming assertive?

_____

_____

_____

What is usually the result of your assertiveness?

_____

_____

_____

What frustrates you the most so that you become assertive?

_____

_____

_____

How did you develop this assertiveness?

_____

_____

_____

Open Aggressive

High scores on this scale suggest that you express your anger through openly aggressive words and behaviors. Open aggression can be viewed as an attempt to maintain your personal values, needs, and beliefs at the expense of others. Open aggressive style includes many aspects of anger including rage, intimidation, and explosive anger. Open aggression, however, can also include criticizing others, bickering and fighting verbally with others.

In what ways do you find yourself being openly aggressive?

_____

_____

_____

In what situations do you find yourself becoming openly aggressive?

_____

_____

_____

What is usually the result of your open aggressiveness?

_____

_____

_____

What frustrates you the most so that you become openly aggressive?

_____

_____

_____

Why have you been unable to control this open aggressiveness?

_____

_____

_____

Suppressing Style

High scores on this scale suggest that you are hesitant to admit your own anger. You have probably decided that the expression of anger is beneath you and not worth your time and effort. When anger-producing situations occur, you put on a good front and pretend not to feel angry at all. You may even say you are surprised that anyone might assume that you are angry. You like to let others think you have it all together and rarely become angry.

In what ways do you find yourself suppressing your anger?

_____

_____

_____

In what situations do you find yourself suppressing your anger?

_____

_____

_____

What is usually the result when you suppress your anger?

_____

_____

_____

What frustrates you the most so that you begin to suppress your anger?

_____

_____

_____

How has this anger management style worked for you?

_____

_____

_____

Passive Style

High scores on this scale suggest that you have a very difficult time standing up for yourself. You tend to have low self-esteem and believe that other people are always right. You may even be afraid to admit that you are angry in most situations. You tend to have trouble asserting yourself with other people. You will give up some of your wants and needs rather than have others criticize you.

In what ways do you find yourself being passive?

_____

_____

_____

In what situations do you find yourself becoming passive?

_____

_____

_____

What is usually the result of your passiveness?

_____

_____

_____

What frustrates you the most so that you become passive?

_____

_____

_____

Why have you been unable to be more assertive?

_____

_____

_____

How to Express Anger Effectively

By expressing your angry feelings in ways that harm and frustrate others, you do not resolve the issue at hand and you prevent a discussion about how to rationally resolve the issue. However, you can learn to express your anger in discussions that lead to a resolution of the conflict situation.

3 STEPS

1) Define the problem so that both parties can understand it.

_____

_____

_____

_____

2) Brainstorm possible solutions.

_____

_____

_____

_____

_____

_____

3) Select a solution on which both parties agree.

_____

_____

_____

_____

_____

_____

Communication Skills

Through effective communication and expression, you will be able to meet your needs and expectations without hurting others. The secret is to learn to communicate so that you express yourself effectively without triggering the anger of the person with whom you are in conflict.

Describe a situation in your life that makes you angry.

_____

_____

_____

How would you typically react in this situation?

_____

_____

_____

What would be the outcome?

_____

_____

_____

How could you communicate your anger in a non-blaming and non-threatening manner?

_____

_____

_____

What solution could you implement to eliminate the problem?

_____

_____

_____

The New Me

Following is a communication format you can use to communicate more effectively with others in situations where feelings of anger are sure to surface.

Describe a situation in your life that makes you angry.

_____

_____

_____

Ask to talk to the other person, but shape and own your message by using "I" and the other person's name (Ex., "Stephanie, I would like to talk with you if you have a moment").

_____

_____

_____

Describe the person's behavior that makes you angry (Ex., "You keep interrupting me when I talk").

_____

_____

_____

Describe how this behavior makes you feel ("When you do that, I feel.....).

_____

_____

_____

Define ways the relationship can be changed to improved.

_____

_____

_____

Ask for feedback about how your message was received.

_____

_____

_____

Anger Expression Style and Trouble

Write about how your anger expression style tends to get you in trouble.

_____

_____

_____

_____

_____

_____

_____

_____

_____

_____

_____

_____

_____

_____

_____

_____

_____

_____

_____

_____

_____

_____

_____

_____

Changes to Enhance Anger Expression Style

Write about how you will make changes to enhance your anger expression style.

_____

_____

_____

_____

_____

_____

_____

_____

_____

_____

_____

_____

_____

_____

_____

_____

_____

_____

_____

_____

_____

_____

_____

_____

_____

Meeting Needs Without Hurting Others

How can you start meeting your needs without hurting other people?

_____

_____

_____

_____

_____

_____

_____

_____

_____

_____

_____

_____

_____

_____

_____

_____

_____

_____

_____

_____

_____

_____

_____

_____

Productive Anger

- Send a clear, non-threatening, message

- Make eye contact

- Listen actively to convey interest

- Stay calm

- Negotiate

Handling Anger Constructively

- Discuss your anger with others

- Discuss your anger with the person with whom you are angry

- Exercise

- Channel your energy into constructive activities

- Change your irrational thinking

- Take several deep breaths

SECTION V:
Anger Consequences

Name_____

Date_____

Anger Consequences Scale Directions

Your anger affects you and all of the people around you. When you become angry, you can damage your work, relationships and health. By better understanding how anger is affecting you and the people close to you, you can begin to manage your anger.

The Anger Consequences Scale is designed to help you identify how significant the impact of your anger is on you and the people who are important in your life and job.

This assessment contains thirty-two statements that are divided into four areas of your life that may be affected by angry behaviors. Read each statement and decide the extent to which the statement describes you.

3 = Very Much	**2 = A Little**	**1 = Not At All**

My anger has been affecting.....

My ability to get work done   3 (2) 1

In the above statement, the circled 2 means that the statement is a little like the scale taker. Ignore the TOTAL lines below each section. They are for scoring purposes and will be used later.

This is not a test and there are no right or wrong answers. Do not spend too much time thinking about your answers. Your initial response will be the most true for you. Be sure to respond to every statement.

(Turn to the next page and begin)

Anger Consequences Scale

3 = Very Much   **2 = A Little**   **1 = Not At All**

I. Work

My anger has been affecting . . .

My ability to get work done	3	2	1
My interest in the work I do	3	2	1
My relationship with my supervisor(s)	3	2	1
How often I am absent from work	3	2	1
My productivity on the job	3	2	1
The number of times I am late for work	3	2	1
My relationships with my co-workers	3	2	1
My relationships with my customers/clients	3	2	1

SECTION I TOTAL = _____

II. Close Relationships

My anger has been affecting . . .

My relationship with my parents	3	2	1
My relationships with my siblings	3	2	1
My relationship with my in-laws	3	2	1
My relationship with my spouse or significant other	3	2	1
My relationship with previous spouses or significant others	3	2	1
My relationship with my children	3	2	1
My relationship with close friends	3	2	1
My relationship with my relatives	3	2	1

SECTION II TOTAL = _____

(Continued on the next page)

Anger Consequences Scale (continued)

3 = Very Much   **2 = A Little**   **1 = Not At All**

III. Community Relationships

My anger has been affecting . . .

My relationships with my neighbors	3	2	1
My relationships with my friends	3	2	1
My relationships with former friends of mine	3	2	1
My relationships with teachers	3	2	1
My relationships with members of the police force	3	2	1
My relationships with people in the community	3	2	1
My relationships with members of local or state government	3	2	1
My relationships with members of religious groups	3	2	1

SECTION III TOTAL = _____

IV. Personal Health

My anger has been affecting . . .

The amount of drinking/drugs that I do	3	2	1
My appetite	3	2	1
The number of car accidents I have had	3	2	1
The amount of tension I am experiencing	3	2	1
The number of headaches I get	3	2	1
My ability to enjoy sexual encounters	3	2	1
Pleasurable activities in my life	3	2	1
My ability to sleep well	3	2	1

SECTION IV TOTAL = _____

(Go on to the Scoring Directions on the next page)

Anger Consequences Scale Scoring Directions

The Anger Consequences Scale provides you with information about the negative effect of your anger in various areas of your life. Add the numbers you have circled for each of the four sections on the previous pages. Put that total on the line marked TOTAL at the end of each section.

Transfer your totals for each of the four sections to the lines below:

SECTION I TOTAL   =   _____ (Work)

SECTION II TOTAL   =   _____ (Close Relationships)

SECTION III TOTAL   =   _____ (Community Relationships)

SECTION IV TOTAL   =   _____ (Personal Health)

Profile Interpretations

TOTAL SCALES SCORES	RESULT	INDICATIONS
8 to 13	**low**	You tend not to become very angry and your anger has relatively little impact on your life and your job.
14 to 18	**moderate**	You show a moderate level of anger and it has some impact on your life and your job.
19 to 24	**high**	Your anger is causing significant damage in your life and your job.

Now is the time to do something about the way that you manage your anger. What has happened in the past cannot be changed. However, you can change the way you control your anger in the future. By taking this assessment, you have identified the areas in your life and your job that anger has hurt you and those around you. To learn more about the effect that anger is having in your life, turn to the next page for a description of each of the four areas on the Anger Consequences Scale. Complete the exercises that follow to help you learn to control your anger more effectively. No matter how you scored, low, moderate or high, you will benefit by completing these exercises.

Anger Consequences Exercises
Scale 1 — Work

People scoring high on this scale often become angry when they are at work. They tend to become angry at their boss and the people with whom they work. They may even begin to become angry with the customers they are serving. They become so angry that it affects their ability to complete work. They end up being less productive and creative than they could be. Their anger may become so intense that they begin to miss work regularly.

How has your anger affected your relationship with your co-workers?

_____

_____

How has your anger affected your relationship with your supervisor(s)?

_____

_____

How has your anger affected your relationship with your subordinates?

_____

_____

How has your anger affected your relationship with your customers/clients?

_____

_____

How has your anger affected your performance?

_____

_____

How has your anger affected your creativity?

_____

_____

Attitude About Work

List the people at work who spark your anger (Josh — your co-worker, Lakisha — your boss, Frank — your employee, etc.). Define what you will do to repair the damage that has been caused through your anger.

People with whom I become angry at work	How I will repair damage caused

Scale II — Close Relationships

People scoring high on this scale become angry with significant others in their life. They tend to become angry with those closest to them including their parents, children, spouse, and significant others. Their anger is aimed at their family and their in-laws. Their relationships with previous spouses may become even more strained due to their anger.

How has your anger affected your relationship with your parents?

_____

_____

How has your anger affected your relationship with other members of your family?

_____

_____

How has your anger affected your relationship with your in-laws?

_____

_____

How has your anger affected your relationship with your spouse, significant other, or EX?

_____

_____

How has your anger affected your relationship with your children or step-children?

_____

_____

How has your anger affected your relationship with siblings?

_____

_____

Attitude About Close Relationships

List the people you have close relationships with and with whom you become angry (Ryan — your husband, etc.). Then list what you can do to repair the damage that has been caused through your anger.

People with whom I become angry	How I will repair damage caused

Scale III — Community Relationships

People scoring high on this scale often become angry when they are with others in their community. They become the angriest with neighbors, friends, and people living in their community. They tend to want to lash out against people with whom they have a community relationship, like members of the police force, restaurant and store owners, service workers and government officials.

How has your anger affected your relationship with your neighbors?

_____

_____

How has your anger affected your relationship with your friends?

_____

_____

How has your anger affected your relationship with members of the police?

_____

_____

How has your anger affected your relationship with people in the community who provide you with a service?

_____

_____

How has your anger affected your relationship with people in the community (churches, temples, and civic support groups)?

_____

_____

How has your anger affected your relationship with government officials?

_____

_____

Attitudes About Community Relationships

List the people in the community with whom you become angry (e.g., Stephanie — the waitress at the coffee shop). Then list what you will do to repair the damage that has been caused through your anger.

People in the community with whom I become angry	How I can repair damage caused

Scale IV — Personal Health

People scoring high on this scale tend to hurt themselves and their physical health because of their anger. They tend to use substances like alcohol and drugs excessively. Their anger may even be increasing the number of traffic violations they have and accidents in which they are involved. They tend to have physical problems like trouble sleeping, headaches and the inability to engage in pleasurable activities.

How has your anger affected the amount of alcohol you are drinking?

_____

_____

How has your anger affected the amount of drugs you use and abuse?

_____

_____

How has your anger affected your driving?

_____

_____

How has your anger affected the recreational activities in which you participate?

_____

_____

How has your anger affected your sleep?

_____

_____

How has your anger affected your physical health?

_____

_____

Attitudes About Personal Health

List personal health problems you are experiencing because of your anger (cannot sleep well at night, etc.). Then list what you will do to repair the damaged that has been caused through your anger.

Personal health problems	How I can repair damage caused

Anger Exercises

The following exercises are designed to help you to thoroughly examine the impact that your anger is having on you and the people close to you.

1. In what situations do you find yourself becoming angry?

    _____

    _____

    _____

2. What is it about these situations that anger you?

    _____

    _____

    _____

3. What situations do you find yourself avoiding because of your angry outbursts in the past?

    _____

    _____

    _____

4. Which situations do you most want to repair the damage you have caused?

    _____

    _____

    _____

5. What angry behavior(s) would you like to change right now?

    _____

    _____

    _____

Anger and Your Relationships

Write about how your anger is affecting you and your relationships.

_____

_____

_____

_____

_____

_____

_____

_____

_____

_____

_____

_____

_____

_____

_____

_____

_____

_____

_____

_____

_____

_____

_____

_____

Aspects of Your Life That Have Suffered

Write about the aspects of your life that have suffered because of your anger.

_____

_____

_____

_____

_____

_____

_____

_____

_____

_____

_____

_____

_____

_____

_____

_____

_____

_____

_____

_____

_____

_____

_____

_____

Relationships That Have Been Damaged

What relationships, if any, do you feel have been damaged beyond repair and why?

_____

_____

_____

_____

_____

_____

_____

_____

_____

_____

_____

_____

_____

_____

_____

_____

_____

_____

_____

_____

_____

_____

Anger Effects in the Workplace

- Lower Productivity

- High Turnover Rates

- Missed Deadlines

- Lower Morale

- Less Creativity

- Chronic Fatigue

- Power Struggles

Anger in Relationships

To resolve a conflict with another person:

- Ask to speak to the other person

- Emphasize the meeting's importance

- Express how you felt at the time of the event and how you now feel

- Focus on what you would like to happen

- Brainstorm and negotiate ways to make it happen

- Ask about the other person's feelings

Substances That Increase Anger and Aggression

- Alcohol

- Nicotine

- Caffeine

- Sugar

- Drugs like marijuana

- Cocaine

wholeperson

Whole Person Associates is the leading publisher of training resources for professionals who empower people to create and maintain healthy lifestyles. Our creative resources will help you work effectively with your clients in the areas of stress management, wellness promotion, mental health and life skills.

Please visit us at our web site: **www.wholeperson.com**. You can check out our entire line of products, place an order, request our print catalog, and sign up for our monthly special notifications.

Whole Person Associates

800-247-6789